CW00956621

Sandy
in old picture postcards

W.B. Hanford

European Library ZALTBOMMEL / THE NETHERLANDS

This second edition was exclusively printed
for 'Bookworms' in Biggleswade. Tel.: 01767-600899.

GB ISBN 90 288 3396 x

© 1986 European Library – Zaltbommel/The Netherlands

Second edition, 2001: reprint of the original edition of 1986.

European Library

post office box 49

NL – 5300 AA Zaltbommel/The Netherlands

telephone: 0031 418 513144

fax: 0031 418 515515

e-mail: publisher@eurobib.nl

INTRODUCTION

Sandy has a long history, mainly of a peaceful and friendly nature, perhaps somewhat servile in early times, for there is little or no evidence of any happening of a warlike, industrial or civil disturbance.

One imagines areas of woodlands, pasture and marshes, some arable land and higher ground in the area of Sandy Hills (or Warren) at Swaden (or Swading) and Chesterfield (now Stratford Road). This must have continued for many years but with the coming of the Romans and Saxons, some forms of culture, law and order, began to shape a community life.

In early English times, Sandy was part of the Kingdom of Mercia, being first occupied by the British Tribe Cassii, but afterwards becoming part of the Domain of Caswallon, becoming Cassivellanus of the Romans. Cassivellanus was a British King conquered by Julius Caesar 54 B.C.

Many articles of evidence of the occupation of the Romans and Saxons have been found by excavation of the Great Northern and London North Western Railways about 1850, in the form of human bones, coins, burial urns, brooches, bracelets, etc. Domesday Book, 11th century, gives the same SANDEIA and Camdens Brittanica, 1586, gives SANDYE or SELENEE. The Parish Church of St. Swithuns records of an earlier date, 1538, gives the name SANDYE. This spelling appears to have continued until 1850 when the letter 'E' appears to have been dropped when the Great Northern Railway was constructed, and the name SANDY has continued ever since.

The Manor of Sandy comprised the whole of the then parish of Sandy excluding Beeston, which was within the Lordship of Beeston. The Manor of Sandy's predominant feature was Sandye Place which was comprised of some 4,000 acres, 100 acres of these including properties were sold at auction in 1851. The Manor, over the years, was dissolved into three manors; Girtford, Hasells and Sandy all of which mainly through the female line came into the ownership of the Pym family of Hasells Hall and still remains today.

Beeston described in Magno Brittania, 1806, as 'another hamlet in this parish on the oppposite side of the river (Ivel) in the Wixamtree Hundred' is a blank space on the Parish Award Map, 1799, marked 'Beeston Lordship'. The Manor formerly belonged to the Abbot of Warden about 1386 in exchange for two manors in Cambridgeshire and became possessed, over the years, by the Thornton and Jeeves families. The Manor was purchased from the Jeeves family in 1956 by the Urban District Council and Sandy Town Council, as successors in title, is now Lord of the Manor in respect of Beeston Green.

Sandy was enclosed by virtue of the Enclosure Acts 1799-1811, establishing boundaries, properties and many related rights. The Award Map was prepared by Edward Gibbons and Edward Arden, and the original map and Award are deposited with the County Records Office.

From a Conveyance of property in 1899 at Beeston Green by Godfrey Thornton, Lord of the Manor, Beeston is described 'in the parish of Northill'. N.B. Beeston was in the ecclesiastical parish of Northill. It is not therefore certain when Beeston became within the parish of Sandy but possibly as an outcome of the Local Government Act 1894 when civil authority, as separate from ecclesiastical authority, was decreed. The area of Sandy is now 4,362 acres.

Sandy was created a Parish Council in 1894, and attained Urban status 1 April 1927, but is now reverted to a Town (or Parish) Council by reason of local government reorganisation 1 April 1974. It is now part of the Mid Bedfordshire District Council. Population figures were: 1931: 3,148; 1945: 3,507; 1955: 3,870; 1962: 3,990; 1963: 4,080; 1964: 4,170; 1965: 4,330; 1966: 4,570. Although these figures show a gradual rise, the percentage increase fell from 11% to 2.2%. There was a steady rise due to the occupation of both council and private dwellings but no industrial or commercial development with a consequence Sandy was becoming a commuter town. The principal industry was for many years market gardening, and is still today, but with agricultural depression and mechanisation, people began to seek employment elsewhere. Many market gardeners went out of business and this also affected other trades.

The Urban Council investigated, in conjunction with the County Planning Committee, the need to arrest the gradual decline and after many consultations an agreement was made with the Greater London Council, under the Town Development Act 1952, for transfer of industry and people from the GLC area to Sandy if they so desired. The scheme started in 1968 and involved erecting 700 houses with 34 acres of industry: 22 acres were added later. In addition, the Urban Authority built a new sewage disposal works, and provided 16 acres of public open space, the Health Authority provided a new Health Centre, and the County Council a new Upper School and Community College plus a new Lower School. There are now five schools with facilities for all ages up to University standard.

The population is now 9,000 (est.). It may be interesting to note that from the creation of the first Parish Council to the dissolution of the Urban Council only three clerks were in office: F.W. Western 1894-1939; H.A. Usher 1940-1956; W.B. Hanford 1956-1974.

There are four established Churches: Parish Church of St Swithun, 11th Century. The most notable Rector among the 42 incumbents is perhaps the Reverend John Richardson M.A. 1858-1913; All Saints Church, Girtford, an annexe to the Parish Church, built 1886, demolished 1980; Wesleyan Chapel, Beeston, 1854; Baptist Church, 1887, original Church (Old Meeting) 1854; Methodist Church, 1910, St. Neots Road — original building in London Road now demolished.

The Victorian and Edwardian eras were particularly noted for the strong community spirit which prevailed and present day residents have much to thank those stalwarts of earlier days. Societies, clubs and organisations of many varieties were in existence, some of which survive today but of a more confined nature. People of all walks of life joined together in activities for the benefit of the community. Names are too numerous to mention but it would be appropriate to remind ourselves of a few; the Pym family of Hasells Hall; the Peel family of Sandy Lodge; E.T. Leeds Smith, solicitor; Alfred Cope; A.G. Jeeves; George Truin; J.H. Mead; G.A. Gregg and many more whose names go down to posterity.

The first fire engine for Sandy Volunteer Fire Brigade, its station and offices over, were raised by deed of gift and public subscription; as was All Saints Church; Nursing Association; Library; War Memorial; part of Bedford Road Recreation Ground and many more projects were augmented by public subscriptions and events such as fetes and bazaars. Although Sandy has grown a good deal, especially in the past 30 years, and the pattern of life has changed, like elsewhere, the community spirit still exists in varied forms and long may it remain. Business concerns, small shops etc. were numerous and of a wide variety; some no longer exist whilst others have developed into larger concerns – supermarkets etc. Records of 1915 and earlier show at least: 4 millers and corn merchants; 4 bootmakers and repairers; 2 fishmongers; 6 grocers; 6 bakers and confectioners; 1 brewery; 6 butchers; 1 ironmonger; 71 market gardeners; 30 public houses and hotels; 3 tailors; 1 coal merchant; 2 dairymen; 1 seed merchant; 4 builders; 4 drapers and milliners; 6 carpenters; 3 hairdressers; 3 stationers, printers and newsagents; 2 cycle dealers; 1 chemist; 1 clock and watch maker; 5 general dealers; 3 dentists; 2 doctors; 1 solicitor; 1 horsedealer; 3 police; 4 blacksmiths; 5 decorators; 1 stonemason; 3 saddlers; 1 wines and spirit merchant; 1 wheelwright; 1 basket maker; 1 auctioneer and estate agent; 1 bookmaker; 4 dressmakers; 1 parish nurse and 1 town crier.

My thanks to all those who have assisted by loan of photographs and in other ways, especially to my daughter Claire, for deciphering and typing my manuscript.

ENTRANCE TO PARK, WATER LANE, SANDY.

1. ENTRANCE TO PARK, WATER LANE. This thatched archway was the gated entrance to the Park grounds of Sandye Place and also incorporated two cottages. The brick wall was the boundary wall between Sandye Place grounds and Water Lane, now re-named Ivel Road. Ivel Road led down to a ford which was a watering place for horses – no longer in existence. This photograph is postmarked 1919 and the archway existed until approximately 1948 when it was demolished for the purpose of building a new Fire Station and training area.

Girtford Bridge, Sandy

2. GIRTFORD BRIDGE. This shows a 'secondary' Girtford Bridge which existed for many years until demolished in the 1950's to make way for road improvements. The bridge spanned a small brook, a tributary of the River Ivel, which flowed under the main Girtford Bridge a few hundred yards west. The bridge carried the original A1 road to the north. Further road works have been carried out and there are now a petrol and service station and a Little Chef restaurant to the right of the picture. Also a roundabout on the A1 dual carriageway has been constructed. The house in the right foreground was Girtford Manor which was demolished in the 1950's to make way for the garage and subsequent roadworks. The street lamp was serviced by gas produced by the Sandy Gas Company.

SANDYE PLACE, SANDY

3. SANDYE PLACE. An extensive view of Sandye Place mansion, part of the parkland and boathouse alongside the river through the Park to the Water Mill about 1900. It is interesting to note that the inland postage was ½d and foreign postage 1d at the time the card was produced. As recorded in the Domesday Book, the Manor of Sandy was held by Eudo Dapifer until his death, in 1120, when it reverted to the Crown who bestowed the Manor to the Beauchamp family. The Manor of Sandye comprised the whole of the parish of Sandy – some 4,000 or more acres – it was later created, probably at sometime before the Act of Dissolution (1536), into three manors, Sandye, Hasells and Girtford. The Beauchamp family held the Manor for 227 years and it passed, through the female line, to Lord d'Engayne. In 1350 Thomas d'Engayne either built or re-built Sandye Place. Practically nothing or little remains of this building but there was a mansion on this site until 1950 when it was acquired by the County Education Committee for Bedfordshire, as a Secondary Modern (now Middle) School. Since 1950 additional buildings have been erected for educational purposes. The mansion and park covers an area of 35 acres.

Interior, Parish Church, Sandy.

4. INTERIOR PARISH CHURCH. This depicts the church interior as it was about 1900. (The card is postmarked 1921.) The marble statue at the end of the choir stalls is of Captain Sir William Peel, K.C.B., V.C., third son of Sir Robert Peel, the famous statesman. Captain Peel, although only 33 years of age when he died in 1858 of smallpox following severe wounding at Lucknow, had a very distinguished naval career particulary during the Indian Mutiny. It was he who purchased the hill, part of Sandye Manor, known as Chesterfield (Stratford Road) on which the younger son of Sir Robert Peel, the Viscount Arthur Wellesley Peel, built the Lodge, now the headquarters of the Royal Society for the Protection of Birds. The statue has now been removed and re-erected in the Memorial Chapel, south transept of the Parish Church. There is a white marble statue to his memory in the Eden Gardens, Calcutta.

High Street, Sandy.

5. HIGH STREET. This view of the High Street, about 1920, facing north represents the south end of the shopping area as it then was. Most of the buildings shown still remain although modernised – mostly by new shop fronts. The foreground building (right) was a public house – The Bricklayers Arms – and a sign (indistinct) can be seen on the front wall of the building. It will be noted that cycles, a motor car, a lorry and a horse and cart all feature in this view.

Park Lane, Sandy.

6. PARK LANE. This is the road leading from the Market Square to Sandye Place and Park – hence its name. This view is probably from about 1920, and the road although not 'made-up' was lit by at least one gas lamp. The cottages were probably 17th or 18th century, now demolished in favour of modern dwellings.

Sandhills, Sandy.

Pub.by
A.E.Nicholls
Luton

7. SANDHILLS (COX HILL). This is the area known as Town Hills and is shown on the Parish Award Map, 1799, to the left of an un-made road named Cambridge Way. Later this was made up and is the present Cambridge Road up to the bridge crossing the main L.N.E. railway lines, built 1850. That part of the road, which is still only partially made up and links with Everton Road and Swaden or Swading is known locally as Green Lane or Lovers Walk. Cox Hill has been owned by the Pym Family for several hundred years and is private. The hill was of sandstone and sand, valuable to the building trade. In the foreground of this view can be seen fencing running alongside, and a gateway over, a railway siding line off the main line. Just over the horizon is Clon Hill, an arable or sheep rearing area, and to the left is the Clay Pond which was originally a pit, dug out for use by the Brick & Tile Works, which existed until 1913/14. In the left background can just be seen the residence of Harry Cope – a local well-known builder, parish councillor and Chairman of Sandy Conservative Club. Sadly the Hill has been removed by excavation, for its valuable sand and sandstone – this occurred after the Second World War when such materials were in great demand for rebuilding following bomb damage particularly in London. The worked out area presents a consider-able bowl and is now an open desolate area.

Lovers' Walk, Sandy

8. LOVERS WALK. This scene shows a footpath which led from the entrance to Caesars Camp to the Everton Road/Swaden (or Swading) Road. The path was raised a few feet above the road or bridleway, but has long since eroded. The tree growth on either side has receded and been cut back in places, and the left side has mainly disappeared. Today the path is seldom used by pedestrians but provides parking space for visitor's cars.

THE SANDHILLS, RD, SANDY

9. THE SANDHILLS ROAD. This is a view of the Sandhills taken from Sandhills Road, immediately over the railway bridge from Cambridge road, in the early 20th century. The name – Sandhills Road – is to some extent misleading, for the road is known locally as Lovers Walk, but there is no doubt of the location. The fencing seen in the foreground has since disappeared and the front area of the hill has eroded – this area is now used by cars. Like the area to the other side of the road – Cox Hill – the Sandhills, also known as The Pinnacle is owned by the Pym family who have leased the area as a public open space of some several acres to the local authority. The Pinnacle, an outcrop of sandstone and sand, rises to approximately 300 feet and commands a splendid view, for several miles, of Sandy and surrounding areas. It was probably for this reason that the site was chosen as a camp site first by the ancient British tribe of the Iceni or Cassii and later by the Romans. As well as a good vantage lookout point the site may have also been used for lighting beacon signal fires.

Sandy Hills, Sandy

10. SANDY HILLS. Another aspect of the Pinnacle probably taken from the Alley Bridge which spanned the main line and branch railway about half way between the High Street and Cambridge Road bridges. The Pinnacle could be approached on foot, via The Alley bridge, over a stile and along a public footpath which followed the line of the fencing which can be seen midway to the right of the picture.

Pine Wood, Old Cambridge Road, Sandy

11. THE PINE WOOD, OLD CAMBRIDGE ROAD. Note the different name once again but the location is quite clear, and but fro the disappearance of some of the trees, remains very much the same today. It is, of course, Lovers Walk approached from Everton Road/Swaden junction facing towards the centre of Sandy. To the left of the picture is the turn-off for the driveway to Caesars Camp House and to the right is Cox Hill.

12. INTERIOR ALL SAINTS MISSION CHURCH, GIRTFORD. This church was erected in 1886 on land donated by Francis Pym at Girtford (later London Road), and served as an auxiliary to the Parish Church. The church seated 200 people and was built at a total cost of £1,180 13s. 11d. £700 of this sum was donated by subscription and the remainder raised at events such as bazaars and public tea parties. The rush seated chairs seen here were later replaced by pews from the Memorial Chapel in St. Swithuns. The small vestry and lectern can be seen to the left, and on the right the organ which may have first seen service at the Victory Cinema, Bedford Road. The church, whose services were mainly conducted by lay readers, was once very popular but became a liability when later it fell into disuse and was consequently demolished 1980. The site has been used for residential development.

Caesars Camp. Sandy.

13. CAESARS CAMP. This splendid view of the house about 1900 was printed in Germany when inland postage was ½d. This view of the front facing onto lawns, gardens and tennis courts typifies the architecture and grandeur of that era. The surrounding area of woodland provided seclusion and privacy and the house is privately owned to this day. In fact a mansion was built on the site of Caesars Camp in 1859 by Capt. John Peel and a William Thurley was engaged to dig for water supply. The mansion was at some time occupied by Francis Pym on his return from honeymoon May 1892. It has since been occupied by distinguished families e.g. Sir Frederick and Lady Liddell Q.C. and presently Mr. Michael Morris M.P.

Hassell's Hall, Sandy.

14. HASELLS HALL. Hasels Manor, formerly part of Sandy Manor, was comprised of the Hall and several hundred acres of farmland. The Hall was built in 1698 by Baron Brittain and inherited by Heylock Kingsley in 1721 who extended the house and grounds. On his death the property passed to his daughter, Elizabeth, wife of William Pym of Radwell, Herts. The estate passed to William on the death of his wife in 1761 and has remained in the Pym family until this day. During the Second World War the Hall was used by the RAF and later was an annexe of Bromham Hospital, Bedford. The Hall suffered from lack of repair but has now been converted to luxury flats. A new house, Everton Park within the grounds of Hasell's estate, has been built and occupied by the Pym family and the surrounding farmlands are managed directly by and for the estate.

15. A typical local gentleman of the late 1890's early 1900's George Thurley seen here walking along Bedford Road. Note the well-trained protected holy hedge abutting the path on the garden boundary of the Broadlands – home of E.T. Leeds-Smith, solicitor, whose offices were and still are next door. The tree and Broadlands still exist but the hedge has long since disappeared to make way for office development for Sandy Building Society (now Gateway).

16. DAVISON'S FARM. This picture about 1920, shows Davison's Farm House, London Road, owned by F.W. Davison & Sons, and in the foreground is William Thurley who was, for many years, farm manager. The farm office was situated at the rear, left, of the house. The farm buildings can be seen to the extreme left and amongst them the onion sheds, which were a distinct feature of Davison's Farm, and where scores of women were employed to peel onions for pickling. William Thurley was a keen bowls player and he played an active role in founding The Sandy Conservative Bowls Club in 1927. Prior to that date the Farm was the venue for bowling events. The house is now occupied as a private residence; its front elevation altered and named 'Folly Farm'.

17. GIRTFORD MANOR. Girtford Manor, once part of Sandye Manor, originally belonged to Caldwell Priory but following the dissolution of monastries it passed to the Crown. Henry VIII gave the Manor to John Burgoyne (1541). A member of the Bromsall family inherited property at Girtford in 1690 and although it cannot be definitely proven it is possible that the family occupied the Manor. The view shows the front of the Tudor designed Manor about 1960 prior to its demolition to make way for garage premises and road improvements.

18. GIRTFORD MANOR. This rear aspect of Girtford Manor when viewed together with the front view (see no. 17) gives a good impression of the house in its heyday with lawns, trees and gardens. There can be little doubt that Girtford Manor must have been the most imposing building in that area of the town. David W. Ibbett and family were the last known full residents of the Manor. Mr. Ibbett owned a draper and milliners business, with premises in the High Street, and his wife, who was an excellent dancer, held dancing classes in the Manor ballroom. The Manor stood empty for some time and fell into a dilapidated state until for a short period, prior to its demolition, it served as a scrap metal depot.

19. TOWN HALL. Although named Town Hall this building has never been used for that purpose. It was built in 1905 by a group of local businessmen, including Messrs. John and Tom Hunt, Henry Hendry, W.J. Blackler and W. Fennemore, who formed the Town Hall Company Limited. Shares and debentures, capital £6,000 and £10 shares were held by various people but very little investment return was made. Until the First World War the Hall was used for dancing and other community activities but during the war it was used by the V.A.D. (Voluntary Aid Detachment) for caring for the injured service men. Following the war the first floor became a cinema and the ground floor the Liberal Club – when shares were sold off the Liberal Club became the principal holder. During the Second World War, and for a time afterwards, the ground floor was used as a Food Office and local National Registration Office. A small room was also put aside for use by the A.R.P. (Air Raid Precautions) personnel. The turret housed the air raid warning siren. In spite of two fires the building, externally, has changed but little and today is used for recreational purposes and managed by the Roundabout Club.

COUNCIL SCHOOLS, SANDY.

20. COUNCIL SCHOOLS. The first local education authority school in Sandy was built in Laburnham Road in 1905/6 and had places for 200 junior and 150 infant schoolchildren. This view shows the infants (foreground) and the girls entrances – the boys entrance was at the front of the building. Although classes were mixed, the boys and girls were segregated, for some years, in the playground.

The Rectory, Sandy.

21. THE RECTORY. Situated adjoining the Parish Church this imposing Georgian house served as The Rectory for very many years. At right angles to the Rectory and parallel with the churchyard wall a range of coach houses were built over which there was a room, used for church functions, called King Alfred's Chamber – later re-named the Rectory Room. The Rectory unfortunately fell into a state of disrepair and despite efforts to preserve the building it had to be demolished in 1962 and subsequently the present Rectory was built on the site. Whilst this work was in hand the Rector lived in a house situated in Bedford Road which had been purchased by the Church to serve as a temporary Rectory. Notable incumbents during the time the original Rectory was in use include: Reverend John Richardson M.A. 1858-1913; Canon A. Sloman; Reverend Strong; Reverend C.G. Hooper; Reverend L.G. Colls, the last Rector to live in the old Rectory; and Reverend D.B.M. Warren, the first Rector to live in the new Rectory.

22. ST. NEOTS ROAD. An ancient road formerly known as 'Tempsford Road', which is one of the town's spinal roads linking Sandy town centre to the A1 north to Tempsford and St. Neots (Cambs.). The route followed by the road has hardly changed since it was shown on the Parish Award Map, 1799. This view about 1900, is taken from the commencement of Carter Street – a short side road serving residential properties and linking St. Neots Road and the A1. It will be noted that there are no made-up footpaths or street lighting but apart from these innovations the scene and the properties remain virtually unchanged today.

23. ST. NEOTS ROAD. This view shows another part of St. Neots Road and was taken some 500 yards south of the previous view (no. 22) and faces towards the town centre. Here again the properties remain virtually unchanged externally. There are now some residential properties on the left between the two lines of trees. Note the telephone pole and wires, the gas street lamps; the school boys' attire gives this view a date about 1920.

BEESTON . SANDY

24. BEESTON. Beeston is a small hamlet within the parish of Sandy, lying on the west side of the River Ivel. No buildings are depicted on the Parish Award Map, 1799, just a blank space marked 'Beeston Lordship'. The picture shows the north end of Beeston astride the Great North Road (A1) in the early 1920's. The Cross public house sign is no longer there and the house, right foreground, has been demolished to make way for the A1 dual carriageway with footbridge crossing just south of The Cross.

LONDON ROAD, GIRTFORD, SANDY.

25. LONDON ROAD. Known for many years as Girtford (and still is by some) this is one of the oldest parts of the town. The road is the Great North Road although the section shown is now by-passed by a dual carriageway to the west. The Kings Arms public house is still in being and was undoubtedly a stopping place for stage coaches on the London/York route. The cottages, typical of working class dwellings, have been demolished. The brick wall, to the right, enclosed Poplar Farm which has also been demolished to make way for private development and a cul-de-sac named Girtford Crescent.

LONDON ROAD, SANDY.

26. LONDON ROAD. Another aspect of the A1, to the north of the town, in the early 1900's, showing thatched cottages now demolished. The red brick building, on the left, was the property of R.G. Oxborough, the grocer, and the smithy is just beyond. The shop has long since been demolished and the site, with adjoining land, is now the offices and industrial premises of BBEA (British Building and Engineering Appliances). Note the gas street lamp and only one footpath. The construction of the dual carriageway through this part of the town (against the wishes of the local authority and local inhabitants) involved the demolition of several properties from the scene shown.

27. Floods were prevalent in Sandy and Beeston and this shows the area most affected – the main junction between Sandy, Girtford, the A1 and the A603 from Bedford. This view shows market garden produce, probably on its way to the railway station, via the floods. The passengers on the pony and trap and the onlookers, from the large house known as Wharf Farm, all seem to be enjoying the situation. Flooding presented a problem for many years (the writer remembers schoolchildren being taken from Beeston to Sandy by horse and trolley, via this particular spot shown, because floods were too deep to enable them to walk). In later years much work has been done by the River Ivel and the Great Ouse Drainage Boards and the problem has been eradicated.

SANDY ALBIONS FOOTBALL CLUB.

SEASON 1920-1921.

Back Row   A. DALTON,   J. DEAN,   J. E. BLAINE,   L. ODELL,   F ODELL   F. JEEVES,   G. TRUIN,   H. W. FINDING,   H. G. FINDING
(Trainer),   (Treasurer),   (Chairman),   (Secretary),

Second Row   A. W. FINDING,   W. FINDING,   F. SPRING,   F. ATHOW   F. CHRISTOPHER
(Captain),

Front Row   A. DALTON,   W. BUTLER,   H. BLAINE

28. SANDY ALBION FOOTBALL CLUB. Sandy Albions are the senior football club in the town (formed 1909) and are based at the recreation ground (formerly known as the cricket field) in Bedford Road. The team shown here was one of the most successful of its day, 1920-21 season, and included Les Odell (alias 'Plonker') who became a professional footballer with Chelsea Football Club for ten years. Also shown is Frank Odell (alias 'Sykes') who despite the disability of a shortened leg was considered the best amateur goalkeeper and wicket keeper for miles around. The club is still in existence at the recreation ground and is now a member of the South Midlands League.

29. A group of local men on the steps of the Victory Cinema, Bedford Road (ground floor of the Town Hall), obeying the call to arms in the First World War. Many of the names will be recalled and remembered: Frederick Huckle, Charles Payne, Frederick Braybrooks, Sidney Braybrooks, Sidney Stacey, Victor Wagstaff, Albert Finding, Frederick Fage, Herbert John Gammons, Herbert George Addison, Clifford Finding and Frederick Spring. Some of these men survived but unfortunately some failed to return.

30. SANDY FIRE BRIGADE, 1894. Until 1948 the Sandy Fire Brigade was voluntary with an organising committee of local men. For many years the Fire Station was on the ground floor of the Parish (later Urban) Council Chamber. The horse-drawn engine, with manual pumps, and the men are all well equipped which reflects the support given by the community and the hard work of the Fire Brigade Personnel. It is believed that the Captain, far right, was Lot Hendry, a local carpenter who despite the beard which gave him an elderly appearance died at the relatively early age of 52. The Brigade held its 20th annual dinner in November 1897 presided over by E.T. Leeds Smith in The Assembly Rooms Market Square. With the implementation of the Fire Service Act 1948 all Fire Brigades came under the control of the County Councils and voluntary Fire Brigades ceased to exist. The fully equipped Fire Station which was eventually built in Ivel Road is still operational.

31. Many will remember this type of early tractor – the harbinger of the demise of the farm horse. This one shown here was the property of George Truin, a well-known member of the community and a market gardener. The tractor was driven by his son, Clifford, and the back inscribed 'Clifford's Tractor' and 'Truins Trusty Tractor Turns Thriving Twitch into Thriving Tilth'.

HIGH STREET, SANDY

32. HIGH STREET. This scene of the High Street, facing north, was taken prior to the 1920's at the confluence of the Railway Bridge and Station Road. The cottage, right foreground, was one of three but has been modernised and now forms part of the whole property. The red-roofed building was the Greyhound Hotel and Stables (now privately owned and the stables still used – an inquisitive horse can often be seen viewing the scene!). The two cottages, left foreground, have been converted into one dwelling and the sign on the end 'Amies Footwear' refers to the shop further down the High Street. The lower roofed building next door to the cottages was the Sandy Gas Company Showrooms, now demolished, and the adjoining building was the Station Temperance Hotel, known locally as the Coffee Tavern. It is obvious some surveying work was being carried out by the group of men on the right but for what purpose is not known. On the far left, just beyond the horse and cart, can be seen the white gable end of 'Green Gables'.

33. This is an excellent view of the south end of the High Street as it was adjoining Green Gables. The row of shops still exists although the nature of trade and the ownership has changed. The row of eight cottages in the right foreground were known as Stone Row, undoubtedly because they were built of local sandstone. The cottages were demolished in 1960 to provide access for the development of the first part of Stonecroft – a Senior Citizens estate.

In the Quarry
Sandy Lodge.

34. The Quarry in the grounds of The Lodge, now the headquarters of the Royal Society for the Protection of Birds, is still in existence and remains practically the same as depicted here, 1905, and is now being used by the Royal Society for the Protection of Birds to form a habitat which will attract the return of sand martins to the Sandy area. The sand martins virtually disappeared from Sandy when their natural habitat, Cox Hill, was excavated and razed to the ground for building material.

35. This picture of the 8th Beds (Sandy) Troop of Boy Scouts shows the Scout Band of 1910. Many of these names and faces will be remembered: front left, J. Eustace (Babs) Blain, band instructor; front right, Albert Saunders and top right, P. Allen A/SM. Others are V.J. Clow, P.J. Rainbow, F.C. Spring, C. Bates, Gus Brawn, R. Judge, J. Ibbott, W. Powers and W. Spring. The Scout movement has always been strong in Sandy and the band, now including Girl Guides, is well-known and prominant at local and national Band Contests and has received many honours. A new fully equipped headquarters was erected in Sunderland Road in the early 1970's.

Girtford Bridge, Sandy.

36. GIRTFORD BRIDGE. A very fine view of this ancient bridge taken from the meadows to the south. The bridge carried the Great North Road (A1) over the River Ivel – now bypassed by the dual carriageway to the east. The bridge was originally constructed of timber but, because of the increase in traffic, was converted to stone in 1780 and soon afterwards became a County Road. The stone used, which can still be seen, was the local sandstone and the same was used for Parish Church and Stone Row Cottages, High Street. The bridge has frequently been damaged as a result of road traffic accidents and in recent years has undergone considerable works of reinforcement; also the gradient has been levelled in order to improve motorist's visibility. In spite of these numerous repairs and improvements the bridge, fortunately, still retains its former character. There used to be a tow path, or haling way, under the bridge for use by horse-drawn boats or barges which used the river for transporting produce – particularly farm produce to the water mills en route.

WATER LANE, SANDY.

37. WATER LANE. A short road leading from the High Street to the ford at the diversion of the River Ivel. An un-named road is shown on the Parish Award Map, 1799, in the same position as Water Lane. There is no record of when the name was changed to Ivel Road but this occurred at sometime between the years of 1872 and 1915. This scene is of the top half, towards the High Street, and remains much the same except that now the road is made-up and footpaths have been laid. The 'Prince of Wales' public house (the sign can just be seen) was de-licensed several years ago. This road also led down to Woolfield – an area of common and meadow land. A footpath, known as The Sandcast, also branches off Ivel Road and connects Sandy with Beeston. Considerable residential development has taken place at the bottom end of Ivel Road during the past twenty years.

SANDY STATIONS.

38. SANDY STATION. This view, mainly of the London and North Eastern Railway, is dated 1904. The line was originally laid in 1850 when, for some reason or other, the letter 'E' was dropped from the old spelling of Sandye. The line was the main London to Edinburgh route; the buildings right, still in existence, were the waiting room, offices and station masters house. At one time it was proposed to close the station (and others along the line) but this was strongly resisted and now the station has undergone considerable improvements, a four line track and the electrification of the line from London is at present being extended through and beyond Sandy. The footbridge gave access to the south-bound track and also to the branch line to the left. Originally the main line was known as the Great Northern and was the first to run through Bedfordshire. It is now used solemly for passenger trade.

39. L.N.W. STATION. Sandy main line station became a very important junction for this branch line which served the East and the Midlands. Originally a local line between Sandy and Potton – a distance of approximately four miles – was constructed by William Peel, son of Sir Robert Peel of The Lodge through whose estate the line ran. Opened in 1857, with much celebration, the line was known as Captain Peel's Railway. This length of line was taken over, in 1862, by a railway from Bedford to Cambridge which was later extended to Oxford, thus linking the two universities. The line was known as the London and North Western, but at some time after 1915 was re-named London Midland and Scottish. It served a very useful means of communication for the local community, to grammar schools Bedford and also for commercial purposes, mainly transporting market gardening produce to market and this was also the case with the main line, which was an important communication link to all parts of the country. But, with the increasing popularity of the car and with the introduction of commercial road hauliers, the line deteriorated and along with many other similar tracks was closed in 1968.

Potton Road, Sandy

40. POTTON ROAD. This road leading from the High Street over the main railway bridge towards Potton – 4 miles – is more or less today as it was defined on the Parish Award Map, 1799. It runs through the Pym estate (left) and the Peel estate (right) – now the RSPB and Economic Forestry Commission – an area of great scenic beauty. The Woodman's cottage on the left is still in existence and occupied, and the brick wall, although somewhat dilapidated in places, still remains. Many elder residents will remember that parishioners were allowed to enter the area enclosed by the wall in the days of depression following the First World War, to gather firewood and many prams – with baby inside – were to be seen laden with wood.

41. MARKET PLACE. The date mark on this card is 1912 but the scene here depicted is of a date much earlier than when this card was produced by C. Thompson of Sandy – certainly before 1910. The buildings and scene of this part of Market Place (now Square) remain virtually unchanged. The public house with sign 'Jarvis Co.' (Bedford Brewers 1873-1910) has since been re-named 'The Lord Roberts', probably at the time of the Boer War 1899-1902 at which he was Commander in Chief. The building on the corner, owned by the Sandy Post Office Company, has been used as the main Post Office up to the present day, but a new Post Office is being prepared by alterations and additions to Ivel Lodge opposite. The entrance to Ivel Lodge can be seen by the trees, now removed. As can be seen, grassed areas were a feature of the Market Place, where small assemblies and a small market used to be held. Some of the elder residents will remember this aspect. The new Post Office which was Ivel Lodge adapted and extended was officially opened on January 17th 1986 by Nicholas Lyell, Q.C., M.P. for Mid Bedfordshire.

EVERTON ROAD AND WOOD, SANDY.   57987

42. EVERTON ROAD AND WOOD. This shows part of the scenic beauty – the wooded estate of the Pym family. Although named Everton Road, the first section incorporating the small group of dwellings was, and still is, named Swaden. From the left turn off Potton Road, the length of the road as far as the link-up from Cambridge Way (Lovers Walk) was named, on the Parish Award Map 1799, as Swading Road. From the link-up point it continued as Cambridge Way but at some time later it was re-named Everton Road – as it is today. The group of dwellings, now modernised, remain but the hedges and trees have long since disappeared.

43. CEMETERY CHAPEL. Situated at Potton Road, Cemetery Chapel was built in 1892 at a cost of £880, by the Parish Council and has remained in the ownership of the local authority to this day. 6 acres of land at £1,200 were purchased for providing a cemetery and two extensions were made in later years; the balance of land being used for allotments pro tem. A caretaker's cottage was also erected and used by the cemetery superintendent until 1980 when it became privately occupied and subsequently sold in 1984. The chapel fell into disrepair and there were proposals in the early 1980's that it should be demolished, but public opinion persuaded the local Council not to do so.

44. SANDY FIRE BRIGADE. No definite date of this picture of Sandy Voluntary Fire Brigade can be given but it is fairly obviously taken just after the First World War. It is taken on the steps of the Town War Memorial in Bedford Road which was erected by public subscription about 1920. Regular uniforms were evidently in short supply, but Captain Jimmy Mead can be recognised by his tunic and peaked cap. In the front row are Harry Hendry and W. Fennemore.

BEDFORD ROAD, SANDY.

45. BEDFORD ROAD. Many will remember this scene of Bedford Road (or Swan Lane as it was known earlier), taken before the post-mark of 1909. The steps to the Town Hall can be clearly seen and also the Conservative Club lower down the road. Note the washing on the line at the Conversvative Club where two cottages existed in what is now the car park. The house on the right was occupied by Sidney A. Fane, who was President of Sandy Show in 1915, and his sisters who ran a private school on the corner of St. Neots Road which became known as Faynes Corner. The house, trees and boundry wall/fencing have long been demolished to make way for road improvements by way of a roundabout to cope with increasing motor traffic on Bedford Road and St. Neots Road, both spinal roads through the town centre, about 1965.

46. HIGH STREET. Another view of the High Street at the corner (left) of the Market Square, which has changed considerably in the past years. The original Red Lion public house (left) has been demolished. A new Red Lion erected on the same site has also suffered the same fate and a supermarket has been built on the site. The building (centre) at right angles to the road was occupied by Horace Sharpe, plumber, painter and decorator. It is now used as an office by W. Jordan & Son in connection with the coal depot at the rear. The stone masons yard and office, established in 1872 by Alfred Hunt, and the shop premises next door occupied by W. Fennemore and those, partly obscured, occupied by W.H. McKelvey are now all demolished. Within the last twenty years the site has been redeveloped for a supermarket with offices over.

47. HIGH STREET. This view shows McKelvey's shop more clearly, in front of which was the premises of Wright & Co., wine, spirit & cider merchants. The premises continued to trade under J.H. Mead but is now an opticians practice. The building right, front, is the Assembly Rooms for many organisations and schooling in early years, it later became a garage with a furniture store at the rear. It is now a sales showroom of luxury bathroom and toilet fixture and fittings. The Procession was obviously on its way to the Parish Church to mark some special occasion. From the sombre dress – although that was the fashion of the day – it seems the occasion was of great importance – perhaps the death of Queen Victoria, 1901 (or Edward VII, 1910).

48. Yet another procession coming sown the High Street towards the Market Square, and awaited by people lining the street. The turning point of the procession is headed by a group of musicians from either the Town Band, Church Lads Brigade or Chapel Boys Brigade. The occasion was most probably the reception of Francis Pym, Squire, and his bride on their return to Sandy on 13th May 1892.

49. This is an excellent picture of the original Red Lion Hotel, with the unusual sight of two elephants outside, (no, not pink!). A characteristic building sadly demolished. The Red Lion meadow, adjoining to the right, was the venue for travelling circuses, repertory companies and fairs. St. Swithun's Feast Week – 15th July – and Sandy Show Week – last Thursday in August – were regular feast days. The meadow was also used regularly for local events and behind the hotel were lawn tennis courts. Sadly the whole area has now been re-developed.

50. GERMAN PRISONERS OF WAR. Here is a group of German prisoners of the First World War with an English overseer (right). These prisoners were employed in cleaning the rivers particularly at Sandy the River Ivel. Some of these men were adept at carving intricate patterns out of the soft bark of willow trees which were used as walking sticks.

51. SANDY CYCLING CLUB. A gathering of members outside The Cross public house on the A1 Great North Road at Beeston. The proprietor of the premises was Charles Single and the date of the fete advertised on the poster is either 1920 or 1926. There are fifteen members shown in this view, fourteen having similar models of cycle with the member (rear, centre) obviously mounted on a penny farthing. Affiliated to the N.C.U. in the 1890's but no longer in existence.

52. SANDY TOWN HALL. Built in 1905 by a group of local business men who formed a company for the purpose of providing premises for local community use – as well as for profit which in the event turned out to be very little. The contractors were Haynes and Fennemore, local artisans, and the architects were Usher and Anthony of Bedford. Other well-known artisans were engaged – Harry Hendry, carpenter; Hunt Bros., stonemasons; who are depicted along with other local workmen also employed on the project. The taking of the photograph was obviously an occasion for the boys.

53. This committee was set up to organise the reception of Francis Pym Esq. and his bride at Sandy on 13th May 1892, on their return from honeymoon.

54. This is the beginning of the procession from Sandy Station on 13th May 1892 on the return of Francis Pym Esq. and his bride to Sandy. The public crowded the approach to the station and when the couple arrived at the Great Northern line they were greeted with loud cheers. The procession was headed by the Band of H. Company Beds Volunteers and the picture shows the Chapel Boys Brigade. 300 schoolchildren carrying flowers, Cricket Club, Tenants, Reception Committee, Fire Brigade and many others, who processed to the Assembly Rooms, Market Square, where the Reverend John Richardson presented an illuminated address to Mr. & Mrs. Pym before all proceeded to Caesars Camp where the couple were to reside. Celebrations continued throughout the evening, ginger beer and ale were dispensed and the church bells rung. An interesting part of the event was the unharnessing of the horses at the station and the carriage was pulled by twenty-four men of the estate all the way to Caesars Camp.

55. This huge bonfire was erected on The Pinnacle of Sand Hill as it was then known overlooking the Great Northern Railway to celebrate the Diamond Jubilee of the reign of Queen Victoria on 22nd June, 1897. The Bonfire Committee members were Sam Osbourne, F.W. Western (Parish Council Clerk), J. Fennemore, E. Marshall, J. Hall, J. Barringer and Mr. Hendry, Estate Steward.

56. A Sunday School class of the Sandy Baptist Church early 1900's. A bunch of likely lads supervised by G.A. Gregg, far right, a Deacon of the Church.

BEESTON GREEN, SANDY

57. **BEESTON GREEN.** This is a small section of Beeston Green which is approximately 11 acres in extent. The freehold of the Green is owned by the Lord of the Manor, which is now Sandy Town Council as successors to Sandy Urban Council since 1st April 1974 on local government reorganisation. The freehold was acquired by the local authority in August 1956 prior to which the successive Lords of the Manor were for several hundred years private individuals. The manorial rights are subject only to certain registered grazing rights which have not been exercised for many years. This view is the north of the Green looking towards the Great North Road, A1, and the house is Beeston Grange. The card is postmarked 1915.

58. BEDFORD ROAD. Bedford Road, looking east towards the town centre from the corner of The Avenue. Formerly known as Swan Lane the road has changed little apart from road and path improvements, the conversion of street lighting from gas to electricity and the demolishment of The Towers (the turret of the Towers can be seen left, rear).

High Street, Sandy

59. HIGH STREET. A grand view looking east which has changed very little over the years apart from a change of occupiers and usage of shops. From the shops of Mead, Ibbett and Illsley it is possible to date this scene about 1890. Only the Post Office still retains its original purpose but this building has now been vacated in favour of new premises opposite.

60. MARKET PLACE. Quite the best overall view of the town centre which was the scene of many public processions, assemblies and events. Late 19th or early 20th century. Sandy Post Office corner can be still seen as can the row of shops at the rear with living accommodation over. The stonemasons yard and office and the shops left, rear, have been demolished in favour of a supermarket development, but the centre buildings still remain. The white distempered premises were then used as a wine & spirit store and are now an opticians. The larger building was the Assembly Rooms, owned by the Sandy Assembly Rooms Company, and used as a place of schooling and meetings. These rooms later became a garage and are now used as a showroom for luxury bathroom fixtures and fittings.

MEAD & SON, PRINTERS, SANDY.

SANDY CHURCH.

61. SANDY CHURCH. A general view of the Parish Church of St. Swithun taken from the opposite side of the High Street. The brick wall still remains but the iron railings were removed during the Second World War by reason of a general government direction and the memorials have been removed.

62. INTERIOR, PARISH CHURCH. This was taken about 1920 showing the statue of Captain Sir William Peel erected in the chancel, today it stands in a side chapel.

War Memorial, Sandy.

111414

63. WAR MEMORIAL. Erected in 1921 inside the Recreation Ground, Bedford Road, with frontage and steps abutting Bedford Road. Provided by public subscription and maintained by the local authority, in memory of the First World War. For many years a Civic Service, in conjunction with the Royal British Legion, was held on 11 November each year at the memorial, but now a Church Service is held on Remembrance Sunday preceeded by a procession of civic heads, Royal British Legion, Scouts, Guides, Brownies etc. headed by the Scout and Guide Band, with a halt at the Memorial for the laying of wreaths.

OLD STONE HOUSES, SANDY.

64. OLD STONE HOUSES. The card is postmarked 22nd December 1908, and used for a Christmas and New Year Greeting. The row of old stone houses was Stone Row Cottages which were built of sandstone about 1860, but were demolished a century later in favour of a senior citizens estated named Stonecroft. The houses either side still remain but the shop and fenced land have long since disappeared about 1946 for the construction of St. Swithun's Way to serve local authority housing estates.

65. ST. NEOTS ROAD. This is a view of the south end of St. Neots Road before the First World War. The building, front, was erected by C.E. Tuppen, solicitor, in 1908 on glebe land for offices and became the office of F.W. Western the first Parish Council Clerk. The property remained as such until 1946 when it became a private residence. The National Schools (later Church of England School and now St. Swithun's Voluntary Controlled Lower School) erected in 1868 can be seen in the background. Roads and street lighting have, of course, improved and the open land has been developed for private housing (1926) and for road access to Windsor Way and other private and local authority development (1946).

66. AERIAL VIEW ABOUT 1925. An early aerial view of Sandy which demonstrates quite clearly the main road system which has changed little until the present day, or indeed when compared with the Parish Award Map, since 1799. It gives a clear view of the market gardening area, open countryside and wooded areas. Many familiar features can be recognised and among them are the following: Parish Church, Baptist Chapel, Conservative Club with tennis courts and bowls green, Town Hall, Council Schools, Church of England School and Market Square. It is also interesting to note just how many of the open fields have been developed and infilled over the years since 1925.

67. SANDY MARKET PLACE. This shows an idea of the loyalty and excitement on the occasion of the Diamond Jubilee of Queen Victoria, 1897. Even the Band of Hope joined in what undoubtedly was not exactly, although orderly, a temperate occasion.

68. Another scene of the same occasion on the Square showing the Assembly Rooms and shops which still remain although in different usage.

69. A group of Sandy Boys/Mens Brigade about 1900, taken probably at either The Towers or Sandye Place. Although a mixture of uniforms and medals can be seen only one instrument of music – a bugle – is evident.

70. GIRTFORD. An old view of Girtford (now London Road) on a stretch of the Great North Road. The Kings Arms can be seen, left, and opposite the public house is a small shop which for many years served as a sub-post office. Poplar Farm, now demolished, is on the right. The elderly gentleman was probably John Underwood of Wharf Farm which was further south.

71. ENTRANCE LODGE, POTTON ROAD. This delightful building is at the entrance to Sandy Lodge and was known as the Swiss Cottage. Believed designed by an Austrian architect – hence the style – and built in the nineteenth century. Acquired by Capt. William Peel (later Sir) 1851 on the sale of part Sandye Place Estate and in due course occupied by Arthur Wellesley Peel (speaker of the House of Commons and later, on retirement, Viscount Peel) whilst The Lodge was being built in 1870. The premises were taken into private ownership when the Lodge estate was sold.

72. BEESTON GREEN. This very old thatched cottage, No. 1 Beeston Green, was originally in the ownership of the Lord of the Manor and on 28th November 1899, was conveyed by William Pawlett and others to William Cooper since which time it has always been a private residence. It is interesting to note that 'this land, cottage and heriditment' was in 'the parish of Northill'. It is included in the list of buildings of special architectural or historic interest. Floods were frequent and the pond was piped and filled-in some years ago.

73. THE MILL. This is perhaps the best overall view of Sandy Mill, showing the sluice gates (four white posts) the stores, the mill itself and the wooden chaff barn as they were in the 1920's and earlier. The arches which discharges water in the Ivel – and still do – when the mill was not working can also be seen.

74. THE NATIONAL SCHOOLS. Later known as Church of England Schools, now St. Swithun's Controlled Lower School. This shows the school as it was when built in 1868, enlarged in 1877 and 1900. The fabric of the original building is the same today and with some improvements the school is still in use. There were two houses attached, one for the headmaster, now a private residence and the other, which can be seen to the right, for the headmistress. The latter now provides an office for the head teacher and a staff room.

75. THE LODGE. Built in 1870 on the south east boundary of Sandy, approximately 1 mile from the town centre, standing in delightful wooded areas of some 104 acres and undoubtedly one of the beauty spots of Bedfordshire. The Peel estate was sold off in 1934 and the Lodge was purchased by Sir Malcolm Stewart who occupied the house with Lady Stewart and family. Sir Malcolm carried out a number of improvements to the house (which externally remained virtually unchanged) and gardens. One of the improvements made was a swimming pool built in the lawns at the rear of The Lodge and it is reputed used by Sir Malcolm every day when in residence. After Sir Malcolm's death, in a few years, the Lodge stood vacant, but in 1961 it was purchased by the Royal Society for the Protection of Birds and it is now the headquarters of the Society. The Society employs well over 125 people at The Lodge and its secondary premises in Station Road, Sandy. Founded in 1889 as a Society to protect against the trade in birds feathers by milliners, it widened its objects in 1891 and became the Society for the Protection of Birds, registered as a Charity and was granted a Royal Charter in 1904. The Society is making an invaluable contribution to bird protection and conservation in this country and other parts of the world.

76. A Sandy Show Committee taken in the grounds of Sandye Place about 1900 certainly before 1913. All but a few can be identified: Alf Banes, J.W. Western, J. Ibbott, W. Dean, F. Brawley, F. Stunt, J. Banes, E. Crawley, A.F. Love, E. Marshall, J.H. Mead, W. Green (secretary), W. Brooks, E. Leedssmith (treasurer), Edward Sills. F.W. Western became secretary 1913. This one day show reputedly the largest one day show in the Midlands ran for 75 years until 1954.